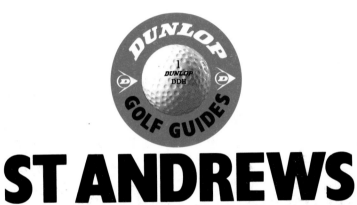

ST ANDREWS

**Sandy Lyle
with Bob Ferrier**

D1089215

World's Work Ltd

First published 1982 by
World's Work Ltd
The Windmill Press
Kingswood, Tadworth, Surrey

Paintings by Ken Turner
Photography by David Pocknell

SBN 437 09066 3

Made by Lennard Books
The Old School
Wheathampstead, Herts AL4 8AN

Editor Michael Leitch
Designed by David Pocknell's Company Ltd
Production Reynolds Clark Associates Ltd
Printed and bound in Belgium by
Henri Proost & Cie, Turnhout

Back cover photograph by
Lawrence Levy

ST ANDREWS

Golf has been played at St Andrews, on the ground of the present Old Course, for more than 500 years. And the Royal and Ancient Golf Club of St Andrews, governing body of the game throughout the entire world with the exception of the USA, has been in existence in St Andrews for more than two centuries. Thus the history and significance of both course and club will be well established in the mind of anyone who goes to St Andrews and claims to be a golfer.

The course may be considered an ancient monument. As such, if for no other reason, it must be preserved. It is certainly an enigma, its tests and its problems varying almost from hour to hour with the fickle changes of Scottish wind and weather. It is rather less a product of nature's evolution than the purists would have you believe. The hand of man has certainly touched it over the decades. It has been condemned as an anachronism, as defying all the philosophies of modern design – and certainly the massive talents of the modern champion professional golfer have overwhelmed it when the course is soft and the weather still.

It is unique. A links course, it is nevertheless different from all other links courses. So for the golfer coming to it for the first time, as perhaps for the man coming to it for the 100th time, some advance preparation is necessary. It is as well to give some thought initially to the nature of the beast. The course runs more or less straight out in a line to the north-west for seven holes, squiggles round a fish-hook loop at the end and runs back to the south-east, with holes 1 to 7 on the way out sharing fairways with holes 12 to 18 on the way in. Most share common or double greens, and the fairways are separated by a central and intermittent line of bunkers, or a slight fall in the ground.

The outward line of the course is protected on the right side by banks of gorse bushes, containing many hidden bunkers, which separate it from the New and Jubilee Courses. The inward line on the right side is mainly defined by gorse, stone walls and disused railway lines, all of which serve to mark out-of-bounds borders and separate the Old Course from the Eden Course. The Old Course is essentially flat. The highest point of the

Tom Morris, R & A professional and four times Open

Champion. His shop still stands beside the 18th green

property can scarcely be 40 feet above sea level.

Yet despite the general flatness there is no more

the 9th and 10th fairways, the ground is an endless ocean of ripples, ridges, mounds, dips, swales, gulleys and plateaux, often carried into the greens and fiendishly splashed with heather and gorse. A man can drive the ball into what he thinks is absolutely the required place and find it some 12 inches above his stance, on a downslope, with a minor mountain in front of him, while only a few yards away is a stretch of perfectly flat fairway offering an open shot from a proper stance.

Thus the course is not fair – but then no great golf course is intended to be fair, no great game is ever fair; so dismiss that from your mind. If you study the place closely and for long enough, you will always find a way. Here are three guiding principles for the average player:

1 For safety, play to the left.
2 If you get into a bunker, *get out*.
3 Never despair.

The right side of every hole on the course is defended by major hazards. The shot to the left is almost always sensible, if conservative, and offers a position from which to advance cleanly.

restless golfing ground anywhere in the world. With the exception of the 1st and 18th, and perhaps

Bunkers on the Old Course are seemingly everywhere. They are very powerful, deep, with high fronts and faces. You must get out first time at all costs, even if you have to play backwards. The course, just as it can consume you in an instant (if you ignore the bunker advice, for example), can also reward you in a remarkably benign fashion for one simple but correct golf shot. So never quit on the Old Course.

The greens also are special. Almost all of them are built up from

Laurie Auchterlonie, the legendary club-maker, and a crowded corner in his famous workshop

the immediate fairway into plateaux, if only two or three feet higher. Many of them fall away from front to back. Many of them have a hollow or a ridge or a mound directly in front of them,

and almost all of them have a bunker, large or small, at the front left-centre – to protect them from the golfer who is approaching from the left. So the Old Course confirms the age-old maxim that golf is not a power game but a point-to-point game; it also sustains the notion that the game and the golf hole should be played 'from the flagstick outwards'.

The player should know where the flagstick is on the green; where he wants to land his ball on the green; the point on the fairway from which to play to the green, and where to drive the ball to get to that point. So, first time out at St Andrews, the best advice I can give is that you should take a caddie. Make sure he is an experienced, local caddie, and not just a bag-carrier.

Robert Trent Jones, the American golf architect, has written: 'The first few rounds a golfer plays on the Old Course are not likely to alter his first estimate that it is vastly over-rated. He will be puzzled to understand the rhapsodies that have been composed about the perfect strategic positioning of its trapping, the subtle undulations of its huge double greens, the endless tumbling of its fairways, which seldom give him a chance to play a shot from a level stance. Then as he plays on, it begins to soak in through his pores that whenever he plays a fine shot he is rewarded; whenever he doesn't play the right shot he is penalized in proportion, and whenever he thinks out his round hole by hole, he scores well. This is the essence of strategic architecture; to encourage initiative, reward a well-played, daring stroke more than a cautious one, and yet to insist that there must be planning and honest self-

The caddie master's office

appraisal behind the daring.'

If you absorb all that and do, at least in part, what Trent Jones recommends, you will walk up that 18th fairway with deep pride and satisfaction no matter how you may have scored.

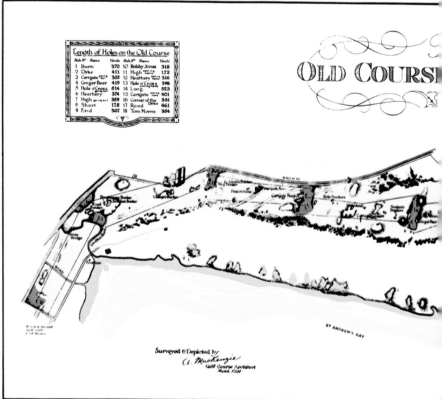

Length of Holes on the Old Course

Hole Nº	Name	Yards	Hole Nº	Name	Yards
1	Burn	370	10	Bobby Jones	318
2	Dyke	411	11	High	172
3	Cartgate	352	12	Heathery	316
4	Ginger Beer	419	13	Hole o'Cross	398
5	Hole o'Cross	514	14	Long	523
6	Heathery	374	15	Cartgate	401
7	High	359	16	Corner of the Dyke	351
8	Short	178	17	Road	461
9	End	307	18	Tom Morris	354

OLD COURSE

Surveyed & Depicted by
A. Mackenzie
Golf Course Architect
March 1924

LOCAL RULES

1 OUT OF BOUNDS (Def 21 Rule 29-1)

(a) Beyond any wall or fence bounding the Course.

(b) Beyond the Swilcan Burn on the right of the 1st hole and in or beyond the trench marked by stakes on the right of the 2nd hole.

(c) Beyond the fence behind the 18th green and 1st tee and on or over the white line between sections of this fence.

Note: The trench on the right of the 12th and 13th holes is not out of bounds.

2 WATER HAZARDS (Def 14 Rule 33)

(a) Those parts of the Swilcan Burn which are unmarked or are marked with yellow stakes are ordinary water hazards (Rule 33-2).

(b) Those parts of the Swilcan Burn to be treated as lateral water hazards are marked with red stakes (Rule 33-3).

3 GROUND UNDER REPAIR (Def 13 Rule 32)

Play is prohibited within a GUR demarcated area; Rule 32-2 applies.

4 ROADS AND PATHS

All roads and paths are integral parts of the Course (Def 20c). The ball must be played as it lies or declared unplayable (Rule 29-2).

5 OBSTRUCTIONS (Def 20 Rule 31)

March stones are immovable obstructions (Rule 31-2).

6 POP-UP SPRINKLER HEADS

All pop-up sprinkler heads are immovable obstructions (Def 20) and relief from interference by them may be obtained under Rule 31-2.

In addition, if such an obstruction on, or within two club-lengths of, the putting green of the hole being played intervenes between the ball and the hole, the competitor may obtain relief, without penalty, in the following circumstances: —

(a) If the ball lie on the putting green, it may be lifted and placed, not nearer the hole, at the nearest point at which intervention by the obstruction is avoided.

(b) If the ball lie off the putting green (but not in a hazard) and is within two club-lengths of the intervening obstruction it may be lifted, cleaned and dropped as in clause (a) above.

ETIQUETTE

Don't play until the match in front is out of range, but don't delay your own game.

If you are overtaken by other players while you are looking for a lost ball, or because of your own slow play, call the other players on, then wait until they are out of range before you continue your own game.

When you've finished putting, don't loiter on the green; there are other people waiting to play.

EMPLOYMENT OF CADDIES

Caddies are not employed by the Management Committee but, for the convenience of players, caddies are permitted on the courses provided they are in possession of a current licence. Caddies must be engaged through the Caddie Master. Do not employ an un-licensed caddie without permission of a course officer or official.

4 BALL: STROKE PLAY IS NOT PERMITTED.
PLEASE REPLACE DIVOTS AND REPAIR PLUG MARKS ON THE GREEN.

LINKS MANAGEMENT COMMITTEE OF ST ANDREWS
GOLF PLACE, ST ANDREWS, FIFE KY16 9JA

Printed in Scotland by Woods (Printers) Ltd., 3/5 Mill Street, Perth PH1 5JB

HOMEWARD PLAYERS HAVE THE RIGHT OF WAY

HOLE	MEN			LADIES				SELF	PARTNER	OPP.	OPP.	+/−	HOLE
	YARDS	METRES	PAR	YARDS	METRES	PAR	STR. ALLCE.						
1	370	338	4	339	310	4	15						1
2	411	377	4	375	343	5	3						2
3	352	322	4	321	293	4	13						3
4	419	383	4	401	366	5	9						4
5	514	470	5	454	415	5	1						5
6	374	342	4	325	297	4	11						6
7	359	328	4	335	307	4	7						7
8	178	163	3	145	132	3	18						8
9	307	281	4	261	238	4	5						9
OUT	3284	3004	36	2956	2701	38							OUT
10	318	291	4	296	271	4	10						10
11	172	157	3	150	137	3	17						11
12	316	289	4	304	278	4	6						12
13	398	364	4	371	346	5	12						13
14	523	478	5	487	445	5	2						14
15	401	366	4	369	337	4	8						15
16	351	321	4	325	297	4	14						16
17	461	421	4	426	389	5	4						17
18	354	324	4	342	312	4	16						18
IN	3294	3011	36	3078	2811	38							IN
OUT	3284	3004	36	2956	2701	38							OUT
TOTAL	6578	6015	72	6032	5512	76							TOTAL
				HANDICAP									
				NETT SCORE									

PLAYER ....

MARKER ....

COMPETITION .... DATE ....

ST. ANDREWS

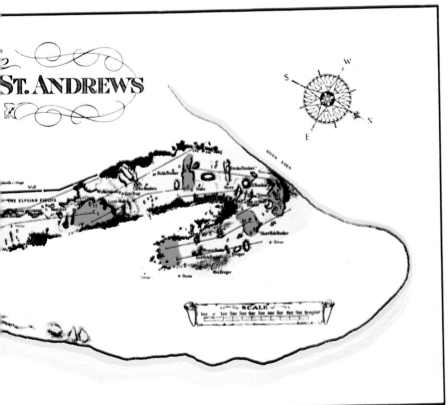

Here you are at last, at the Mecca for golfers. As you stand on the huge teeing ground, behind you is the old, grey clubhouse with its tall, ground-floor windows; the long sweep of St Andrews Bay reaches off to the right; the golf shops and houses and Rusack's Hotel form file down the left. Before

you is a vast expanse of fairway, embracing the 1st and 18th holes, a double fairway surely 150 yards across without a single bunker in sight. Your first problem will be to stay sufficiently relaxed and in control of yourself for the shot in hand. You will be well aware of where you are, and the whole ambience can be overpowering, no matter how often you stand on this first tee. You will be well aware that the clubhouse behind you is more than 100 years old, that the Royal and Ancient Golf Club which inhabits it is more than 200 years old, and that golf has been played here or hereabouts for the best part of five centuries. In fact you would be a poor golfer indeed if all of this did not give you a twinge or two.

I have some consolation for you. The first hole of the Old Course is just about the easiest opening hole of any championship course anywhere. You have a flat, abundant fairway to aim at. Granny Clark's Wynd, a narrow metal roadway, crosses the fairway about 130 yards out – no problem. The main characteristic, in fact the only characteristic, of this hole is the Swilcan Burn, which crosses the front of the green hard by the putting surface, then turns and comes back part of the way up the right side of the fairway. The presence rather than the perils of this burn preoccupy the golfer, and it has produced some adventures for the best of them.

In the 1970 Open Championship, Tom Shaw of America putted

his third shot, from the back of the green, all the way into the burn. He then dropped a ball under penalty on the far side of the burn, and promptly chipped back over it onto the green and directly into the hole – score 5! In the same championship Doug Sanders pitched into the burn with the second shot of his first round, and scored six on the hole. Yet he almost won the championship, missing a three-foot putt on the 72nd hole which brought him a losing play-off, decided again on the very last green, with Jack Nicklaus.

The only danger on the drive, once you have your nerves and concentration under control, is the right side, where an out-of-bounds fence runs all the way along. If you hit the ball

The 1st tee and the Royal and Ancient clubhouse

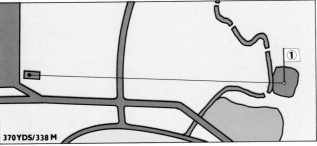

370 YDS/338 M

too far (!), the side sector of the burn might just be in play. So drive to the left, on the left corner of the green. You can aim even further left, on the bridge over the burn, if you prefer.

With the pin in the centre of the green, in fact anywhere but at the front, you have a perfectly straightforward, orthodox shot to it. In still air, if you have driven the ball out a bit

more than 200 yards, you will have a mid-iron to play. If the pin is at the front, which could mean only five or six yards from the edge of the burn, ignore it. Go for the centre or back of the green, where there is no trouble.

The essential point is to start your Old Course round sensibly. Knock the drive down that wide fairway. Pop the second to the middle of the

green. It is quite big enough for anyone to hit. Take your two putts and settle for a comfortable par, and compose yourself for the adventures ahead.

What's in the name?

The burn or stream is the Swilcan Burn which loops round to guard the green.

Go for the centre or back of the green to avoid possible trouble

The 1st Green and the Swilcan Burn

OLD COURSE
HOLE NO. 2
DYKE
411 YDS.
PAR 4 STR. 3

The Old Course and Carnoustie, above all other links courses, can be disquieting in particular respects. They have so many flat tees, so much broken or dead ground that it is often difficult to know how far or where to go, quite apart from how to get there. This is not so much a question of blind shots as of blind lines, and in knowing on what precise line the ball should be hit, particularly from the tees. The second at St Andrews is a vintage Old Course hole, and your first real introduction to the variety of hazards and variations of routes that have to be considered on this extraordinary golf course.

The second tee is hard by the first green and is quite flat. For the first time we meet a long bank of gorse which guards much of the right side of the fairway and marches out in a line all the way to the 7th hole and the end of the course, separating it from the parallel New Course. Like all these outward holes, the 2nd is something of a driving hazard.

All the same, I would not be too fidgety about your drive. There is a

Above:
The ridge hiding the green

Bunker divides the 2nd and 16th greens

Ridge protects the right side of the green

2nd shot at the 2nd

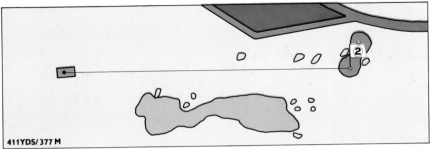

411YDS/ 377 M

reasonably wide fairway to find, with the line to the left of the whins (gorse). There is a bunker on the right side, about 130 yards out, with two little pots beyond it, at around 180 yards. On the left, between the 2nd and 17th fairways, is the bigger Cheape's bunker, 250 yards away, and if your driving line bisected that right bunker and Cheape's, you would be in an excellent position. The line of the teeing

ground itself should keep you right.

The second shot is the main challenge on this hole, and is perhaps one of the most difficult on the course. The nature of the green makes it so. It is long from left to right, the first of St Andrews's famous double greens, and is coupled with the 16th. It is probably as much as 55 yards across, with its twin. A bunker at the front, eating into the putting surface,

'divides' the second from the 16th, and the right half, which we are concerned with, has a ridge dead in front of it. The green behind that ridge slopes away, and in fact a slight rise towards the back of the green, stiffened by the Wig bunker, gives the green a hollow effect.

The ridge is more pronounced on the left, and if the flagstick is to the left, you will not see all of it. You would then have to pitch the ball short, and hope it runs up and over the ridge onto the green. With the pin to the right, everything is much more open, and this underlines one of the basic tenets for playing the Old Course, which is that the tightest driving lines are down the right. These also happen to be the more dangerous driving lines. If you can drive down a tight line along these whins on the opening holes, and avoid the bunkers, which are scattered, almost all of them hidden, amongst and beyond the whins, you are likely to be in a good position. On almost every hole on the Old Course, the right side of the fairway, with access to the easier right side of the greens, is the more rewarding place to be.

Provided you find the right side of the fairway,

your second or approach shot will be a good deal less risky. If you have any doubts about making the distance on your second, aim for the right-front corner of the green. If anywhere, that is the area in which to be short. Despite a good deal of undulation in the ground there, you have a chance to chip the ball close with your third.

There are two big bunkers, not always easy to see, on the left some 70 yards and 40 yards short of the green. Most of the ground in front of the green is undulating, and your best bet, as ever, is to fly the ball if you can all the way to the putting surface. If you cannot, hope for a bit of luck in getting a decent lie and stance for the third! And don't be embarrassed, ever, at St Andrews, by luck: everyone who plays this course will need some, and everyone who plays the course can expect some – both good and bad.

What's in the name?

The dyke marked the boundary of the railway property, now owned by the Old Course Hotel.

Long bank of heather and gorse

The 3rd hole follows the pattern of the 2nd, but although substantially shorter, it is perhaps progressively more difficult, certainly on the tee shot. It too illustrates a basic tenet, this time of golf architecture: the more the player takes advantage of the safe or easy way on shot A, the more complicated should be the subsequent

challenges on shot B.

Again, there is not a lot to see, no clearly defined target, as you line up your drive. You could safely follow the line of the teeing ground and aim for a point 20 yards inside, or to the left of, that persisting border of whins. Alternatively you could go well to the left, out towards the Principal's Nose bunkers on the

adjoining 16th fairway, which are about 190 yards from your tee, but the more left you go, the tighter your second shot will be.

The adventurous driving line is again down the right, just inside the line of gorse, but hidden along that right side is a minefield of bunkers from 170 yards to 240 yards, any of which can be penal. The

On this hole there is no clearly defined target from the tee

Never expect a true bounce in these bumps and hollows

Approach shot must pitch on the green and hold

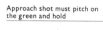

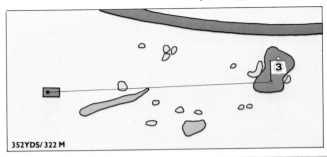

352YDS/322 M

optimum line might be just on the right of a central fairway bunker, 120 yards out.

A series of ridges runs in diagonally across this fairway, from 10 o'clock to 4 o'clock, advancing from the left and the 16th fairway. These make for, at best, uneven stances on your approach shot, which poses stiff problems, as at the 2nd hole. Here, the green is rather deeper, from front to back, but with an entrance very much nipped in by the huge Cartgate bunker hard by the putting surface on the left. This green also has a pronounced slope from left to right. There is a mass of uneven ground in front of it, and in there you will be entirely at the mercy of the

bouncing ball.

The further right you have driven, the more open the second shot will be, but that will mean you have flirted with pot bunkers and banks of gorse. The further left you have driven, the more into play will come that big Cartgate bunker, closing out pretty effectively the left half of the green. And if the hole is cut behind Cartgate, as it would be at least once in every championship, for example, then the shot required will be quite fearsome.

If the pin is at the right back, you will probably not see the bottom of it, even when you are only 20 yards short of the green, so strong are the slopes and contours. There is a

small bunker at the back of the green, just to complicate your complications. But such a mass of difficulties often produces simple decisions. You must drive carefully here, on line, and hit a decent shot. You should then be playing a pitching club with which, at all costs, you *must* hit the green.

The real difficulty here, as everywhere on the Old Course, is in not quite knowing where to go, and not being able to see. Even second or third or fourth time round, you will not know exactly where the humps and hollows are, and where you can land the ball safely and where not. You must never really expect to get a straight and true bounce here.

And you must not allow yourself to become impatient with this golf course. Don't rush it. Let it all come to you; it will, in time.

What's in the name?

This refers to the gate in a cart track which led out towards the Eden estuary, and was used by fishermen.

OLD COURSE
HOLE NO. 4
GINGER BEER
419 YDS.
PAR 4 STR. 9

The first thing the average player should do here is take a careful look at the yardage. This hole can be a puzzle, and much depends on the conditions. For instance, I can imagine a first-class amateur playing it, in still air, with a drive and an 8-iron. On the other hand, in air that is less than still, it can be two woods, particularly in cold weather or with the wind against. So the average player should realistically deem it a par 5 and play it accordingly.

It is a long hole, but at least we can see the green, or at any rate the flagstick, far ahead down the line of the teeing ground. This line is hard along the right side with its now customary perils, but again it is the more adventurous line, and will give a better view of, and better access to, the green on the second shot.

In a sense the Ginger Beer can be likened to a valley, running between the higher ground to the left along which the 15th hole runs, and the 'wall' of gorse to the right. But it is not exactly a quiet, pastoral valley. Several

The direct line appears to run through a valley

Mounded fairway ridge defending the green

Approach to the 4th

419 YDS/383 M

Wall of gorse on the right

ridges enter from the left, from the 15th, and out on the left side of the fairway is what I can only describe as a hump. Many people tend or elect to drive over there, and if you were planning to hit a massive hook anywhere on the Old Course, this might be the place to do it. Nowhere are you guaranteed a level lie for the second shot on this fairway, but if you can get beyond the ridges and beyond a big bunker on the right, the back of which is 220 yards from the tee, you might be lucky since the fairway opens out there into a reasonable area, and gives you some comforting space to work with.

From there, as you contemplate your second shot, you are faced with a mounded fairway ridge defending the green, a good distance short of it but five or six feet high. Past this ridge, the ground is nothing but humps and hollows all the way to the putting surface.

The green is quite big. Although present, no bunkers are to be seen, the reason being that none is effectively in play. There is the usual big one, front left, bisecting the double green, and just short of this a trio of 'Student's' bunkers, none of these really in line. What there is to perplex you is the mound or ridge short of the green. If you can carry that, you should never be too far from the centre of the green. If you feel you cannot carry it, play just short of it, favouring the right – your ball will probably break to the right in any case. From that little corner you can attack the flagstick fairly well. But note that the green is long, a good 40 yards, with firm folds in it. If you do hit the green with your second, you may still be facing a long putt which will need a good deal of work, so the clubbing on the second shot is very important, and the accuracy of the chip shot, if you need one, no less so.

What's in the name?

In the last century one Daw (David) Anderson had a ginger-beer stall; it must have been a memorable brew.

OLD COURSE
HOLE NO. 5
HOLE O' CROSS
514 YDS.
PAR 5 STR. 1

Hole o' Cross (Out) is the first of only two par-5 holes on the Old Course. It runs beside and contra to the other, the 14th or Long Hole on the inward half of the course.

The drive here continues to pose problems we have faced on the earlier holes, with the

The view from the tee emphasizes the need to play to the left

line of gorse running down the right side, past the Pulpit bunker which is about 150 yards out, and concealing beyond it no fewer than six bunkers of varying size but equal ferocity – deep and very straight-faced. These range from 200 yards to 255 yards, so you *must* keep the ball to the left of that line. There is plenty of room to go left, and the man who draws the ball will have an advantage here. But for first-timers it poses again the question of exactly where to go. The perfect line in still air would be just to the left of that Pulpit bunker. There is a stone marker down there, which is exactly the place to hit.

The left side is interesting. Here we are probably at the narrowest point on the course, not

much more than 100 yards across the joint 5th and 14th fairways, yet there seems plenty of room to the left of that driving line – further evidence that nothing is simple at St Andrews. The 14th fairway is higher than the 5th, and an escarpment of three or four feet in height lines the left side of this hole. Inside it, the ground is very uneven, falling, tumbling, making a level stance unlikely. However, if you could possibly get your drive out 250 yards or more, along that left line, you might well run into a level area of fairway. If the course is dry, if you are down-wind, if you hit your best shot, it would certainly not be impossible.

Almost every shot on this course calls for decision-making, and the

second shot at the 5th is no exception. You will be faced with a high ridge crossing the entire front of the green, with only the white flag itself showing above it. Two bunkers are set into this ridge, rather like The Spectacles on the 14th at Carnoustie, but set wider apart. The ridge is approximately 410 yards from the medal tee. Immediately in front of it is a piece of honest, level fairway which should give you a good stance and lie. If you carry this ridge with a good, positive shot, you might well be on the front of the putting surface; the ground beyond the ridge is reasonable, and will certainly move the ball forward *unless* the big gulley behind the ridge smothers the ball.

If I say you can

High ridge containing two bunkers crosses the front of the green

2nd shot at the

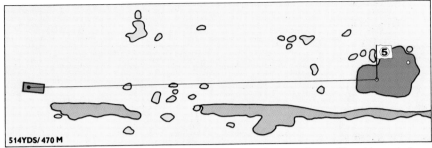

514YDS/470 M

consider this a birdie hole, choke back your surprise. You must think positively and optimistically on this course. If you are downwind, which means with a south or south-east wind, it need not be beyond your talents.

So now we come to the point of decision. Can you carry that ridge comfortably? That depends on your drive, your lie and stance, the wind and the weather and your shot-making. If you think you can do it – go ahead, do it. Don't think defensively. The line would be right between the bunkers or marginally left of that. If you have any doubts about making the carry, don't think defensively, think tactically, and play short of the ridge. That will almost certainly give

you a good stance and lie and leave you a third shot, a pitch of 120–130 yards to what may appear the biggest green on any golf course that you have seen. If you are into a headwind, of course, your decision will probably be made for you – you will have to play short. But if you are short of the ridge in two, for whatever reason, walk forward to the top

of it, and have a look beyond. That might be just as important as anything you do on this hole.

What's in the name?

Probably a reference to a cross that once stood here rather than any crossing of the course.

For safety on the 2nd shot aim for a patch of level fairway short of the ridge

OLD COURSE
HOLE NO. 6
HEATHERY
374 YDS.
PAR 4 STR. 11

At first glance, this looks no more than a hit-and-hope job. Immediately in front of the tee there is nothing but a mass of gullies, gorse and heather,

with a path snaking somewhere through it. It all underlines the value, first time round, of investing in an experienced caddie.

The line of the teeing ground here seems to me to be slightly too far to the right of the ideal line, and I think your direction should be on the hangars of the RAF station at Leuchars in the distance, across the estuary of the River Eden.

Still the bank of heather and gorse runs along the right, rising now, with a more powerful appearance. Again there is the cluster of bunkers, four this time in the range 210 yards to 230 yards on the right

side, which you will not see. On the left are the two very big Coffins bunkers, perhaps 200 yards away. Between the Coffins and the right-hand bunkers is (by St Andrews standards) good fairway space. So if you had your drive out 220 yards or more on my line, you would be 150 yards or less from the middle of the green and in a good position for the approach shot. Downwind, in dry conditions, your best shot could take you really quite close to this green.

As always on the Old Course, the green demands the closest attention and concentration. The problem here may well be holding

the green with your approach, or at least getting decently close to the flagstick. There are not too many greens on this course which rise nicely to the back to hold your shot, with completely clear, uncluttered entrances. This time there is no screening ridge compromising the front; instead, a dip or gulley runs across. This then rises quite quickly to the putting surface, which in turn slopes away from you.

The green is long from left to right, quite deep from front to back, and most of it, certainly the right half, can be clearly seen. Given a

The 6th – Heathery

good drive, you might
like to consider running
the ball on, hitting a low
shot with, say, a 6- or
7-iron, pitching the ball
perhaps 30 yards short of
the putting surface and
taking a chance with the
bounce. In any event, you
do have some options
with the second shot. It is
the drive, and getting the
right driving line, which
provides the major
challenge on the hole.

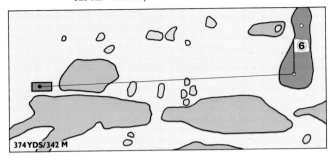

374YDS/342 M

What's in the name?

In former times the
heather grew abundantly
here, though there is less
of it now.

The fairway ridge hides
bunkers to left and right

Green slopes away at the back

Cluster of bunkers at 210–250
yards

2nd shot at the 6th

OLD COURSE
HOLE NO. 7
HIGH
359 YDS.
PAR 4 STR. 7

HOMEWARD
PLAYERS
HAVE RIGHT
OF WAY

A view from the tee of the
adventurous direct route

Working out your driving line is your first problem. In front of the tee, and quite close to it, is a large heather-covered bank which makes the drive blind. Pressing in on the right, thankfully for the last time, is our now-familiar line of gorse bushes, but this time instead of ignoring it and in general playing away from it, we can make it an ally. Beyond this frontal high ground, we play into the only zone that passes for a valley at St Andrews, at least until we get to the 18th. It is a wide expanse of fairly true ground where the 7th hole and the short 11th cross. From somewhere in that area, we then have to play to possibly the most complicated green on the course.

If you take the shortest, most direct and most adventurous – and also the best – route to this hole you have to drive along the line of the gorse on the right, almost clipping the bushes. On that line you will have to carry 220 yards to be safely in the valley, but a solid hit on that line can put you in the perfect position for your second shot. A more conservative line would be to hit directly over the bunker on the bank or hill in front of the tee. That bunker is 170–180 yards from the medal tee, and there is some 20

The Strath bunker

The 7th green from the Right-Hand Rough

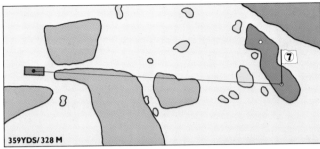

359YDS/328 M

yards of bad ground behind it.

When you come over the hill, the prospect is unique. The 11th and 7th greens form yet another of the Old Course's famous double greens, the 11th occupying the left part, and the 7th with its white flag – your target – to the right. This double green is probably the longest from left to right, if not the largest in area, on the course and lies 'across' the approach shot on the 7th, running from 8 o'clock to 2 o'clock. If you have driven to the left, your approach shot will be longer but will be played more down the length of

the green. The huge Cockle bunker, some 20 yards short of the putting surface, is on a direct line tee-to-green and covers the front (it is driveable by supermen provided the conditions are right).

The bunker to the left of the Cockle digs right into the putting surface and is usually taken as marking the extreme left of the 7th, and the extreme right of the 11th, in target terms. So if your drive has been 'straight', on the more dashing line along the whins, you will be closer to Cockle and the green, but will require a different approach shot –

shorter, but probably higher, a softer, holding pitch into a green running across the shot.

When you come to look at this green more closely, you can hardly imagine it existing anywhere but St Andrews. It slopes quite severely downwards from its left, or if you prefer back, and falls away at the back, or to the right, towards the 8th tee. There are ridges and rises at the very front of the green which you must carry. In fact at the front of the green, actually on the putting surface, there is first a slight dip, then a quick rise up to the plateau green proper. In addition,

there is a spine running through the green, so that the factor of luck, as the ball pitches and runs along it, is great. If the ball should come to rest in the wrong place, a good deal of hard work will have to go into the putting. The second shot must therefore be very positive, from whatever angle, and aimed to pitch on the putting surface.

What's in the name?

The most mountainous sector of the baffling undulations that give the Old Course so much of its character.

The huge Cockle bunker

Green falls away at the back and on the right

The most direct, though adventurous, line is tight on the right

OLD COURSE
HOLE NO. 8
SHORT
178 YDS.
PAR 3 STR. 18

The Old Course has but two par 5s and two par 3s. This is the first of the short holes and in yardage it is not too forbidding, although it can play very long into wind (south-east). Billy Joe Patton, the famous American amateur and Walker Cup player, has told how he played this hole in successive rounds, when the wind changed course, with a 2-iron ('Ah hit that bawl with every bone in ma body') and then an 8-iron ('Ah jes' tried to bleed it a little').

The green doubles

Above:
The Short Hole bunker

The Short Hole bunker is well short of the green

The short 8th

The 8th – Short

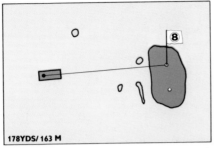

178YDS/ 163 M

with the 10th. It is very big and quite long from left to right, and frankly it is hard to miss. The hole has but one real routine defence, the Short Hole bunker, slightly off the centre line to the left and a long way short of the green. There are modest grass banks which disguise the front of the green to some extent, and club selection is obviously important here.

The 8th is probably the first really unsubtle hole on the course, and you really must make par or better here. We are now into The Loop, which does exactly what it says. From the 7th hole to the 11th, the course loops round in a fishhook so that, come the 12th tee, we are now pointed back towards the town on a run of holes which parallel directly the first half-dozen outward holes.

Holes 8, 9 and 10 are perhaps the easiest on the course for various reasons. They are all flat and open, without blind shots, set out plainly before you with every-thing to be seen; all are on the short side, and there is very little undulation in the ground. One advantage is that they give the player a period of rest and recuperation, without forbidding challenges, before the major problems ahead on the final third of the course. Even more important, they can be used to hold the score together. Holes 7 to 12 have been played in successive threes by more than one golfer, and even the average player must score relatively well, certainly from 8 to 11, to protect his card.

The 8th could never be called a severe hole, but it has to be tackled with some care. The main danger is under-clubbing.

What's in the name?

Here at the top of the 'loop' is the first of the two short holes on the course.

OLD COURSE
HOLE NO. 9
END
307 YDS.
PAR 4 STR. 5

This hole is entirely flat, straight-forward and straight-away, with everything visible from the tee. The fairway is very wide, and is shared with the 10th hole, rather like the 1st and 18th. Here a few bunkers and occasional light rough separate the two and give them at least some definition.

The 9th gives you plenty of options, or

Boase's bunker and the End Hole bunker narrow the approach to the green

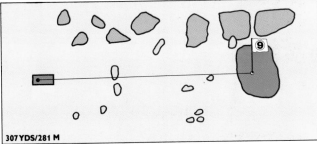

307 YDS/281 M

more accurately plenty of margins, on the drive. A pair of cross-bunkers called Kruger, not much more than 100 yards away, lies directly across the fairway. The driving line from tee to centre of green would take you over the gap between these two bunkers. You should aim slightly to the left of that point. If you took the dead-centre line you might well finish in the End Hole bunker, which is 240 yards from the tee and 70 yards from the centre of the green on

the direct line. Short of, and wider than, the End Hole bunker is Boase's bunker, which can catch a sliced shot.

There are two large bunkers in the left rough, one about 170 yards from the tee (Mrs Kruger), the other just wide of the left front of the green; but neither should be in play and the End Hole bunker should only be a problem on the drive.

The second shot, yet again, is testing, but not for a typically St Andrews

reason. The single green is very big, very flat, and is simply an extension of the fairway. This makes the second shot rather difficult to judge. Depending on your position, you may have to pitch the ball all the way to the hole, or pitch and run it there, or give it the old 'Musselburgh scuffle' – all the way along the ground. Indeed, if you have driven the ball well in good conditions, you may even think of putting from off the green.

Tony Jacklin, in his freakish round in the 1970 Open Championship, holed out in two here for an outward half of 29, with a shot that might well have gone over the green, but instead whacked the flagstick and fell into the hole!

What's in the name?

The 9th green marks the end or turning-point, and the beginning of the long walk home.

Large flat green and flat approach

End Hole bunker at 240 yards

From the 9th Tee

OLD COURSE
HOLE NO. 10
BOBBY JONES
318 YDS.
PAR 4 STR. 10

This is the return hole, very like the 9th, and in common with it increases in interest and character the closer you get to the green. There is a trio of bunkers only just in the left rough 100 yards out. The straight line from tee to green will be directly over them. You will see the End Hole and Boase's bunker on the right, and the Kruger bunkers in the distance. None of these should concern you, but just beyond Kruger and to the left is a 10th-hole bunker some 240 yards from the medal tee. That bunker, provided you do not drive into it, is a good driving line, or preferably a little to the left of it. You would then be driving at the midpoint between that bunker and the trio on the left. This is your best driving line, and it also gives you a good deal of margin.

What's in the name?

A tribute to the great American amateur, whom some rate as the greatest player in the history of golf.

The 10th Green

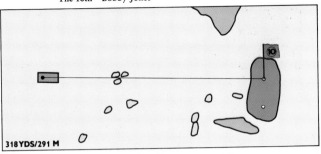

318 YDS/291 M

Unlike the 9th hole, in the general driving area here, say over the final 100 yards to the green, the ground is undulating. The green is raised slightly at the front, and then slopes away from you and to the left. This is the green which is twinned with the short 8th. All kinds of approach shots are 'on', though all pose slightly stronger problems than at the 9th. If you go for the full-blooded pitch, it might be difficult to stop where you want to on the green. If you decide to run the ball, then stance, lie and the contours of the ground between you and the green will make the shot intriguing. So once again this old course remains in character. Even on its easiest holes, which so far you might judge to be 1, 8, 9 and 10, there is always a puzzle, however minor, for the player.

The green, too, undulates a good deal more than the part which serves the 8th hole, and there are some definite borrows to be coped with. But since this is a very short par 4, anything more than par on the hole can be counted a failure.

Left:
Undulating ground in front of the green

Green is raised slightly at the front and slopes away and to the left

The 10th Hole bunker

OLD COURSE
HOLE NO. 11
HIGH
172 YDS.
PAR 3 STR. 17

This is one of the world's greatest, most celebrated and most demanding short holes, regardless of conditions. It is the most clearly defined target on the course, yet also the most clearly and powerfully defended.

The green is very narrow from front to back. It slopes upwards severely, then falls over into a rough-strewn bank, down to the estuary of the River Eden, and you can consider that a disaster area. At the front, it is resolutely defended by the very large, very deep Hill bunker on the left, and by the smaller but equally vicious Strath bunker on the right. These are possibly the two most fearsome bunkers on the course. The entire contouring of the area short of the green, and the very front portions of the putting surfaces, will gather shots towards these bunkers. And since we are at the end of the course, on the brink of the Eden estuary, there is almost always some wind, and since the green is totally exposed on that sharp slope, it is always inclined to be fast. That is more than

Above:
The Strath bunker and
the steep sloping green

The Hill bunker

The Strath bunker

From the 11th Tee

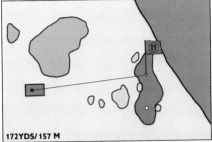

172 YDS/ 157 M

enough to make the 11th tee a terror tee, a real danger point on the Old Course. Anything pitching 20 yards short is likely to break towards the Strath bunker. Go over the back of the green, and you will be pitching out of strong, tangly rough onto a slippery downslope.

There are nevertheless some tactically sound points to be made. Regardless of pin position, you should try to be at the front of the green, so that you have an uphill putt to the flag. And if possible make sure that, if you are going to need a second putt, it too is directly uphill. Side-hill putts on this green take an unbelievable amount of borrow. If the hole is cut directly behind either of the frontal bunkers, aim instead for the front centre of the green. On the whole it is better to be short than over the back. If you do get into one of these deep traps, *get out*, first time, even if it means playing backwards to the fairway.

This is a very demanding par 3. If you score more than that, do not let it upset your composure. Gene Sarazen, one of the few men to have completed golf's Grand Slam, and who was both Open Champion and US Open Champion in the same year, once made six at this hole – including three shots in Hill bunker.

What's in the name?

The short 11th shares its relative heights with the 7th, which it crosses.

OLD COURSE
HOLE NO. 12
HEATHERY
316 YDS.
PAR 4 STR. 6

The Heathery is a tricky, fidgety hole, getting its name no doubt from the heather banks on the left which spread away in front of the 7th tee. It is a short par 4, and for this and other reasons it presents many problems, for the long hitter in particular. From the high tee by the 11th green, above the estuary, there is a positive stew of bunkers on the straight line to the green.

The key factor dominating the drive is the big Stroke bunker,

dead ahead in the centre of the fairway 175 yards out. Another smaller bunker is set just past it and slightly wide of it. A pair of bunkers, unseen from the tee, backs it up at 215 yards. Thus the strategy requires you to go wide of Stroke on either side.

The green is very narrow, only some 15 yards from front to back, and it rises abruptly into a shelf. There is a single bunker 40 yards short on the direct tee-to-green line, and the ground immediately in front of the green is very uneven. The optimum shot to

Uneven ground in front of the green

Approach to the 12th

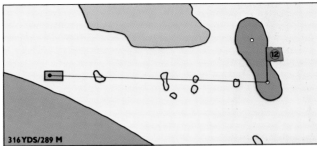

316 YDS/289 M

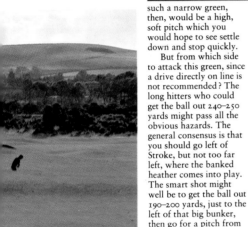

The approach from the
left directly over
the bunker

Narrow green but no trouble
behind

such a narrow green, then, would be a high, soft pitch which you would hope to see settle down and stop quickly.

But from which side to attack this green, since a drive directly on line is not recommended? The long hitters who could get the ball out 240–250 yards might pass all the obvious hazards. The general consensus is that you should go left of Stroke, but not too far left, where the banked heather comes into play. The smart shot might well be to get the ball out 190–200 yards, just to the left of that big bunker, then go for a pitch from that side. This would give you rather more of the length of the green to work with.

Mercifully, there is no trouble over the back of the green, so the pitch shot can be over- rather than under-clubbed. If you go well wide to the right of Stroke, where there are no hazards as such, you are into very uneven ground, and pitching to the narrowest of greens. Even on this short par 4, there are enough complexities to illustrate what a unique golf course it is. Whether you care for it or not, you have to agree that it is uncommon!

And by the way, from the tee, just about the most distant point on the course, there is the most wonderful panorama of the Eden estuary, the rolling hills above the Leuchars road, and the well-loved prospect of the distant, 'auld grey toon'. Take a moment to savour it, before you set out on the long, hard road home.

What's in the name?

Heathery (In) gets its name from the heather which runs along the left-hand side of the fairway.

OLD COURSE
HOLE NO. 13
HOLE O' CROSS
398 YDS.
PAR 4 STR. 12

This is the first of a run of five holes, from 13 to 17, which collectively form the main single challenge of the Old Course. In general, they run in a south-easterly direction and so are most likely to be running across the prevailing wind, a right to left wind. With the possible exception of 15, all are very severely restricted by subtle or substantial hazards, natural or otherwise, and all of them demand resolution on the part of the player – clear thinking, correct decision-making, positive shot-making, too, but above all resolution in facing up to the demands these holes make.

The structure of Hole o' Cross (In) is quite marvellous. There is a wide dense bank of heather and gorse running down the right side for most of the hole. About 220 yards from the tee, it branches left into what I can only call a range of foothills, which cross the fairway and continue in front of the 6th tee, the parallel hole, and create the blind tee shot which is experienced there. Down the centre line between the two fairways, and establishing more or less the left side of the 13th, is a parade of bunkers of various sizes. Thus our first thought on the 13th tee is of driving into a rectangle confined by the gorse on the right, the bunkers on the left, and the 'foothills' at the end.

Probably the first governing factor here will be the playing conditions. Into a head-wind, this hole will play very long, and in some circumstances even a professional player will need two woods. The first bunker, Nick's, is only 120 yards out. Behind it on the left are the Coffins, two very big traps covering the range 150–190 yards. Beyond them, at the left end of the cross ridge, is another pair, Cat's Trap and Walkinshaw's, about 260 yards out.

There are three options on the drive:
1 You can drive straight ahead into the rectangle. You should not go more than 200 yards. Beyond that you may dribble into the foothills.
2 You can go directly over Coffins. You should not then go more than 240 yards or you will be flirting with Cat's Trap.
3 You can go positively left of Coffins. You should not then go more than 240 yards, or you will be tangling with more foothills.

The second shot brings no relief from decisions, decisions. The three drive placements have one thing in common. They demand a second shot which is all carry. The ground to the green is so badly broken that the approach shot cannot possibly be landed short with any hope that it will run truly on. The direct route, from drive 1, is effectively closed out by the Hole o' Cross bunker, dead in front of the right half of the green and hard into the putting

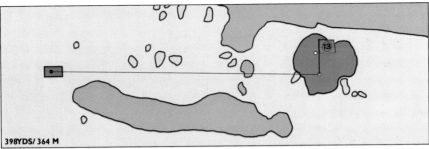

398YDS/ 364 M

surface. The best bet here, even if it does seem a touch cowardly, is to aim for the left half of the double green, on the white flag marking the 5th hole. Otherwise you might well be saddled with a shot of 180 yards which would have to carry well into a huge green.

If you have gone left, or followed either drive 2 or 3, you have diminished the threat of Hole o' Cross bunker, and will have a slightly shorter shot, but it will be essentially the same shot in that it must carry, and you should still favour the white flag on the 5th green.

There is just one possible escape route if you have taken the drive 1 route, and if you are not sure you can make the distance on the second shot. To the right of that Hole o' Cross bunker, to the right of the green and towards the 14th tee, is a piece of perfectly fair ground. You might think of popping your second over there, then chipping to the flagstick. However you make par here, it is a par well made, and if you are one over, fret not. As you see, it is a hole of unrelenting perplexity.

What's in the name?

Hole o' Cross (In) shares its name with the 5th hole and the cross is thought to have stood by the shared green.

Broken ground right through to the green

Foothills cross the fairway at 220 yards

Approach to the 13th

Far left:
The view of the foothills from the tee

right. The line should be on the spire at the right-hand end of the distant town. Needless to say, you cannot see the green from the tee, but when you do, you will find that it is very big, and can be attacked from a variety of angles.

Although you cannot see them very clearly, it is essential that you pass the Beardies to the right, staying between them and the wall. If you have driven up level with them, or slightly past them, you will have entered the Elysian Fields, perhaps the only piece of honest, ordinary, recognizable fairway to be found beyond the 1st and 18th. The Elysian Fields extend perhaps a couple of hundred yards towards the green. At the end of them, the ground closes in from both sides in yet another tangle of broken, unreliable ground with heather and foothills and so on, which persists for a

This is potentially the most destructive hole on the course. In Open Championship play, Gene Sarazen and Bobby Locke have scored 8, and Peter Thomson 7. Gary Player was once in one of the Beardies bunkers and declared that it had not been raked 'since it was made', which we can suppose was rather a long time ago.

The 14th is a long, sapping hole, demanding three fine hits from a professional player (you will be asked for three shots averaging 175 yards from the medal tee). So the thing to do is stand still for a moment, get your breathing right, give some thought to what you are about, and take a long hard look at the thing. Having said that, I must tell you that you will not see very much!

A stone wall squeezes into the fairway from the right, before turning back outwards again. It marks an out-of-bounds line. The first hazard on the left side is the Beardies, a set of bunkers making, with the angle of the wall, a rather narrow gap. The Beardies comprise one large and three small traps extending from 160 yards to 200 yards from the medal tee. In a left to right wind, the narrow gap between them and the wall makes this a terrifying drive to get

further 100 yards almost to the green. There are two small bunkers along the left side, Benty and Kitchen, but dominating the scene, and the tactics from now on, is a huge and famous bunker, apparently as big as a tennis court – the very properly named Hell.

For a long hitter who has got one of his very best shots out well past the Beardies, the choice may be simple. He can go for an enormous smash past Hell, but again it will have to be his very best shot. For the

average chap, who perhaps has hit a good drive of say 225 yards, and is in a good position, the choice is not so easy. He will then be 180 yards from the centre of Hell bunker and 300 yards from the centre of the green! One thing at least he can be sure of: if he is playing into wind, he has absolutely no chance of carrying Hell bunker.

The conservative player will knock the ball forward, 100 yards or so, towards the end of the Elysian Fields, and go for a third shot of about 170

It can be sensible to use the full width of the double green

Hollows in front of the green

The Approach to the 14th and Hell Bunker

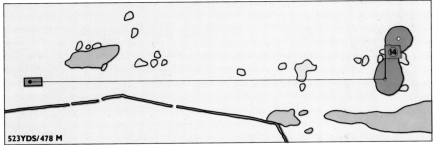

523 YDS / 478 M

yards to the green. Another obvious possibility for the same man is to blast the ball straight over Hell, if he thinks he can make the carry. He should be warned, however, that some 80 yards beyond Hell – and out of sight, of course – are other traps, principally Grave and Ginger Beer, protecting that line and the left half of the green.

Happily there is a well-established third course, used often by the best of players. It is to play the second shot to the left, aiming a good 50 yards to the left of Hell bunker, into the lower 5th fairway, and taking a line on the white flag on the 4th green. There is good ground there, more or less level with the leading edge of Hell bunker, and you have a fair chance of a decent stance and lie for what might be a mid-iron or long pitch shot to the green. A sensible line to keep your par within reach, even on the third shot, would be on the white flag, and reckon on getting down with two

solid putts from there.

Although the double green is broad from left to right, the 14th green has hollows in front from which it rises steeply up a frontal bank, then falls away to the back quite sharply, so that many approaches will go all the way to the back, or even off the green. People also have trouble putting up and over that rise to the flag, if the approach has been left short. You must forget here, as at so many other Old Course greens, the business of running or bumbling the ball on.

The 14th is a critical hole. You must play it deliberately, using sensible tactics for the conditions, and above all, you must keep the ball in play. All those bunkers – Beardies, Benty, Kitchen, Hell, Grave, Ginger Beer – are penal. Get in any of them, and you have certainly lost one shot.

What's in the name?

Long *is* long, and is made longer by its most evil traps – Beardies, Benty, Kitchen, Hell and Grave.

OLD COURSE
HOLE NO. 15
CARTGATE
401 YDS.
PAR 4 STR. 8

Into wind, this can turn into quite a longish hole, demanding two good hits. However, on a still day, it is a drive and moderate iron to a big green and altogether a much more simple hole than the others on this inward half. If you can relax anywhere in this stretch, it may well be here.

Along the right side of the hole is the usual file of gorse, although towards the green the old railway line comes into view on the right, but is not, I think, in play. As the railway appears, the gorse fades out, and you will be relieved to know that, from that point on, you are once and for all finished with gorse. On the left side, the big Cottage bunker starts about 140 yards out and leads off to the left. Beyond it, and hidden, at 200 yards' range, is the sneaky little Sutherland pot bunker. The driving line is to the right of Cottage where there is fair space, aiming on that same church spire in St Andrews town (see 14th). This should bring you to a flat area of fairway, and if your drive gets nicely along into a slight gully between mounds, you will be in a perfect position for a confident thrust at the green.

About halfway to the green on the second shot, more or less on line, is the trio of Rob's bunkers, but they should not concern you. As usual at St Andrews, the left half of this green is guarded by a pot bunker, but again the green is huge, and will take three or four clubs' difference from front to back. This and a good deal of dead ground in front of the green make club selection on the second shot very important. I would be inclined always to take one club more than it looks.

Finally, it should be said that the fringe of the green, at the immediate front and right side, is altogether more friendly than you have come to expect on the Old Course. The ground is reasonable. You will have a fair chance to chip or putt from off the green close to the flag, and although there is not one single hole on this course which you dare not respect, I would guess that there is more pleasure from less hard work to be won from the 15th than most.

The huge double green with its solitary pot bunker

The 15th – Cartgate

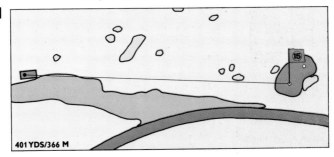

401 YDS/366 M

Left side of the green is
guarded by a pot bunker

Green is huge and it is easy
to under-club the 2nd shot

2nd shot at the 15th

OLD COURSE
HOLE NO. 16
"CORNER O' DYKE"
351 YDS.
PAR 4 STR. 14

This is one of the most dangerous holes on the course. The disused railway line runs hard by the tee, all the way along as far as the green; it closes off the entire right side of the hole, since it marks out-of-bounds. A group of three bunkers, Principal's Nose, is slightly left of the direct line to the flag, covering 170–190 yards from the medal tee, and leaving the narrowest of gaps – it looks little more than 15 yards across – to the railway line. And past Principal's Nose, 40 yards on, is Deacon Sime bunker, placed to trap anyone who flies directly over that trio of hazards.

The ambitious driver can have a go directly for the green, between these traps and the railway. This makes for a shorter, easier second shot into the green. It also requires an act of cold courage, or, if you prefer, an act of madness. It is difficult to imagine anyone tackling it in a hard left-to-right wind.

The alternative way is to go left of Principal's Nose, or on a line directly over the left bunker of the three, which should keep you wide of Deacon Sime. About 230–240 yards out on that line is a friendly fairway, but from there the line of the second shot is compromised by Grant's bunker, 20 yards short of the putting surface, and Wig bunker which eats into the left front of it.

The green itself, as usual, is raised on a plateau, with devious little gullies in front and at the back, and the ground just short of it tends to throw everything to the right, towards the railway fence. The ground between the right side of the green and the railway fence is fair, but there is not a lot of it – only a few feet.

In the 1978 Open Championship, Simon Owen and Jack Nicklaus came to this hole together in the last round, Owen leading the championship by one stroke from Nicklaus. He nailed a long drive down the right side, on the more dangerous line, and at a time like that, at the very climax of the champion-

ship, it took a lot of guts to do it. Nicklaus drove to the left. Then Owen, over-excited no doubt, hit his approach over the green, chipped back, and missed the putt. Nicklaus pitched on – and holed his putt. So the Open was lost and won, with a swing of two strokes on this 16th hole. It is that kind of golf hole, a short par 4, but with its variety of challenges and options a very subtle hole indeed.

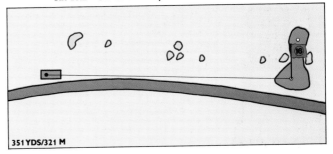

351 YDS/321 M

What's in the name?

The green is tucked into the corner of the dyke which also gives its name to the 2nd hole.

Devious gullies in front of the raised green

Old railway line runs beside the green

The 16th Green

Left: The out-of-bounds fence following the old railway line

OLD COURSE
HOLE NO. 17
ROAD
461 YDS.
PAR 4 STR. 4

Debatably the most famous single hole in the entire world of golf, the Road Hole for most golfers most of the time is a monster, and your first time on the 17th tee, even if you are a seasoned player, will induce a moment of terror. The hole is rated a par 4, yet for any club golfer it must be a 4.5, and in any conditions save quite still, it should be considered a par 5.

The siting of the tee and green, rather than any particular ground hazard, make the hole an absolute freak. Surely no one could imagine that a modern architect, even in a nightmare, could conceive of such a design. The point is that the 17th hole was not designed in the modern sense, but that like so much else on the Old Course, it 'happened'. It should be said, though, whether the

purists like it or not, that all these bunkers did not grow out of rabbit scrapes and sheep hollows; I'm sure that man has had much more of a hand in the development of the course than we sometimes allow.

Nevertheless, to make any sense of the present 17th, we must look back a little. In a course plan of 1821 for example, when the holes were played 'the other way round', the present ground was used for a perfectly straight, and dare I say normal, hole. Later in that century, when the railway came to St Andrews, sidings and sheds were built along the side of the 17th fairway. With the 17th tee hard by the 16th green, in the 'corner of the dyke', these black sheds impinged strongly on the fairway from the right, demanding a totally blind drive over them which became inevitably both famous and notorious. One wonders why the tee was not advanced to the corner of the sheds, making the hole shorter but at least allowing the player to see where he was going. On the other hand, not seeing the fairway or the green is not unusual on this course.

After the coming of the sheds, there were

many ploys among St Andrews caddies as to the line of the day, depending on the weather – slightly left, right, or directly over the gable of the sheds. In the late 1960s, when the railway and the sheds had gone and the present Old Course Hotel was built, the hotel people built an open trellis fence which maintained the profile and the roof outline of the black sheds, but at least gave the player some slightly better clue as to where he should go. A low stone wall and a path mark the edge of what was railway property, and which now belongs to the hotel.

The first problem, that of the drive, remains. From the corner of the 'sheds', the fairway turns to the right. The test is just how much, if any, of the corner should you cut off? Playing straight-away, or slightly to the left of the corner, you could well overrun the fairway and be in the rough between the 2nd and 17th fairways. You would certainly be left with a hopelessly long second shot. Playing too far to the right might leave you caught up in the grounds of the Old Course Hotel. The carry over the corner is in fact much less fearsome than it may look, even today. Indeed you could drive quite close to the hotel

building with a good shot and be well over the angle and into clear fairway. In all of this I have made no mention of wind or playing conditions, but you must be sure to apply them to your deliberations.

Given a decent drive into the fairway, you still must face a long shot – the hole is only 14 yards short of the regulation par-5 distance. And you will be looking a long way forward to the most infamous green in golf. It is set diagonally across the shot, built up into a very positive plateau three or four feet above the fairway, very long from left to right, very narrow from front to back. At the left centre, the viciously deep Road Hole bunker bites into the green so voraciously that there are putting surfaces on either side of it (and players of the very highest class have been known to putt into it). Immediately behind the back putting surface the green falls down a bank to a path and then a metalled road with a stone wall on the other side of the road. A pin position behind that bunker can be positively evil, and over the years this hole and this green have produced an endless series of triumphs

The approach to the green from the bunkers on the left of the fairway

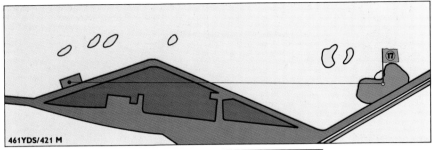

461 YDS / 421 M

and dread disasters.

In terms of modern thinking and modern techniques, the hole can be considered unfair in that such a green is positively not designed to receive a shot of 200 yards, which most players will be playing to it. However, the hole exists, you are not allowed to pass it by; it is a very powerful, challenging hole for anyone of ability, and we have to get on with the playing of it.

The tactics on the hole, despite all this, are straightforward. You must drive cleanly into the fairway, over the corner. You must hit your second shot quite deliberately short, as close as you can to the front-right corner of the green. At St Andrews they tend to water the approaches and the front fringes and this upslope, so you should have a soft bounce, and not much forward run on the ball. You must keep well to the right of the Road Hole bunker and you must *not* go over this green. If you do, you may never get back onto it. From that position, short right, you can chip or pitch along the length of the green (a shot which demands more than usual care because of the contouring) and be well content with two putts if you should need them.

This is a very, very powerful hole and a real cardwrecker. In any championship, there are more fives and sixes than fours scored here. In fact in the last round of the 1978 Open Championship, I believe there was not one single birdie made at the 17th hole.

What's in the name?

A metalled road runs directly behind and beside the putting surface.

Viciously deep Road Hole bunker

Metalled road and wall immediately behind the green

The 17th Fairway from the Corner

H ere you are at last, after all the sweat and effort, and no doubt many a new golfing experience, back at the world-renowned scene – the vast acres of the twin 1st and 18th fairways; the Swilcan Burn and its little stone bridge under your nose; Granny Clark's Wynd crossing 220 yards out; the houses and clubs and hotels behind the white fence along the right side, and the mass of the Royal and Ancient club-house looming ahead.

You have two things to think about. First, you may well be tiring, the legs feeling heavier, the reflexes a little duller. Second, you may again be influenced by the immediate surroundings, by the history of the place and the scatter of people leaning over the rails by the green – they are always there – with their implied criticism of everyone coming up this last fairway. So first of all relax, take a couple of deep breaths on the tee, and swing a shade more easily. And second, I would say, find a bit of swagger, have a bit of confidence in your own game and to hell with anyone around the green – you are just as likely to be better than they are at 'the gowff'.

And I have some cheer for you. This is not a difficult hole. It is an easy hole. If you drop a stroke here, it is not a stroke lost, but a stroke squandered. On the drive, the one thing that can go wrong is a slice out of bounds, over the fence. That is un-thinkable. Aim for the clock on the Royal and Ancient clubhouse and let it fly out there. Granny Clark's Wynd is approximately 120 yards from the centre of the green, and if you are in the general area of her metal path, you will be pitching the ball. Be bold.

The 18th green, scene of many famous victories

The 18th from the Swilc

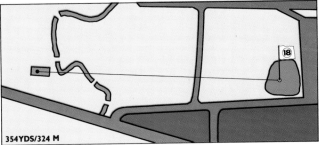

354 YDS/324 M

Go for the centre of that huge green. This hole is at its most difficult played downwind, with the pin cut at the very front of the green.

On the second shot, you have to handle the only real problems on the 18th – the green itself, and perhaps the Valley of Sin. This is a wide hollow immediately in front of the left half of the green. If you are hitting a full pitch to the green, it is no problem. Fly the ball over it. If you have

driven the ball rather a long way over Granny Clark's Wynd, you may want to play a running shot to the green. In that case you must give the ball enough weight to run through that sinful valley, and up onto the putting surface.

The green is enormous, sloping from right to left and down from back to front, with the back right-hand corner very much higher than the rest of it. It is the biggest single green

on the course, and putting it and its impish borrows will demand your final effort of concentration on this extraordinary Old Course. There it is – you have done with it. Only one thing is certain from your experience. You will want to come back, and play it again, for any one of a hundred different reasons.

What's in the name?

He was the famous old R & A professional and greenkeeper.

Granny Clark's Wynd runs through the fairway at 220 yards

Enormous green with its own hazard – the Valley of Sin

Since Prestwick relinquished its exclusive grip on the Open Championship, the Old Course at St Andrews has been dominant, from Tom Kidd in 1873 to Jack Nicklaus in 1978. It remains the dominant name in world golf, the place where all the great champions love to win.

1
DUNLOP
DDH

Course Record (Old Course)
65 Neil Coles
(Open Championship 1970)

Open Championship

1873 Tom Kidd	179	1921 Jock Hutchinson (USA)	296
1876 Bob Martin	176	1927 R T Jones (USA)	285
1879 Jamie Anderson	169	1933 Densmore Shute (USA)	292
1882 Bob Ferguson	171	1939 Dick Burton	290
1885 Bob Martin	171	1946 Sam Snead (USA)	290
1888 Jack Burns	171	1955 Peter Thomson (Australia)	281
1891 Hugh Kirkaldy	166	1957 Bobby Locke (S Africa)	279
1895 J H Taylor	322	1960 Kel Nagle (Australia)	278
1900 J H Taylor	309	1964 Tony Lema (USA)	279
1905 James Braid	318	1970 Jack Nicklaus (USA)	283
1910 James Braid	299	1978 Jack Nicklaus (USA)	281

Alcan Golfer of the Year Championship
1967 Gay Brewer (USA) 283

Alcan International Championship
1967 Peter Thomson (Australia) 281

Dunlop Masters' Tournament
1949 Charlie Ward 290

Martini International Tournament
1962 Peter Thomson (Australia) 275

PGA Championship
1979 Vicente Fernandez (Argentina) 288

PGA Match Play Championship
1954 Peter Thomson (Australia)

Scottish Open Championship
1973 Graham Marsh (Australia) 286

Spalding Tournament
1947 Henry Cotton   1948 Norman von Nida (Australia)

Amateur Championship

1886 H G Hutchinson	1930 R T Jones (USA)
1889 J E Laidlay	1936 H Thomson
1891 J E Laidlay	1950 F R Stranahan (USA)
1895 L M B Melville	1958 J B Carr
1901 H H Hilton	1963 M S R Lunt
1907 J Ball	1976 R Siderowf (USA)
1913 H H Hilton	1981 P Plojoux (France)
1924 E W E Holderness	

Commonwealth Tournament
1954 Australia

Eisenhower Trophy
1958 Australia

European Amateur Team Championship
1981 England

St Andrews Trophy
1976 Great Britain

Walker Cup

1923 USA 6	GB 5	1938 USA 4	GB 7	1971 USA 11	GB 13
(One match halved)		(One match halved)			
1926 USA 6	GB 5	1947 USA 8	GB 4	1975 USA 15	GB 8
(One match halved)				(One match halved)	
1934 USA 9	GB 2	1955 USA 10	GB 2		
(One match halved)					

Ladies' Amateur Championship

1908 Miss M Titterton   1965 Mlle B Varangot (France)
1929 Miss J Wethered   1975 Mrs N Syms (USA)

Commonwealth Tournament (Ladies)
1959 Great Britain

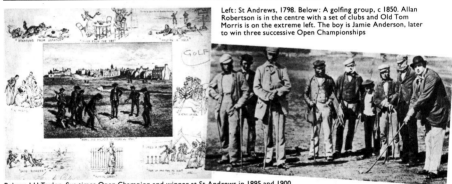

Left: St Andrews, 1798. Below: A golfing group, c 1850. Allan Robertson is in the centre with a set of clubs and Old Tom Morris is on the extreme left. The boy is Jamie Anderson, later to win three successive Open Championships

Below: J H Taylor, five times Open Champion and winner at St Andrews in 1895 and 1900
Right: Bobby Locke, Open Champion in 1957, surprised everyone by breaking into song at the presentation ceremony

Top left: Peter Thomson ends his first round with a long putt on his way to the 1955 Open Championship. Top right: The only time two trophies have been presented to the Open Champion – Kel Nagle winner of the Centenary Open in 1960 received a replica trophy to mark the occasion. Centre left: Open Champions gather at St Andrews in 1970. Back: Arthur Havers (1923), Gene Sarazen (1932), Dick Burton (1939), Fred Daly (1947), Roberto de Vicenzo (1967), Arnold Palmer (1961, 1962), Kel Nagle (1960), Bobby Locke (1949, 1950, 1952, 1957), Henry Cotton (1934, 1937, 1948), Peter Thomson (1954, 1955, 1956, 1958, 1965). Front: Denny Shute (1933), Bob Charles (1963), Max Faulkner (1951), Jack Nicklaus (1966, 1970), Tony Jacklin (1969), Gary Player (1959, 1968). Gary Player (1974) and Jack Nicklaus (1978) have both won the Open for a third time since this gathering. Centre right: The victorious Great Britain team, winners of the 1971 Walker Cup. Standing (l to r) Warren Humphreys, Rodney Foster, Michael Bonallack (capt), David Marsh, Charles Green, Hugh Stuart, Roddy Carr. Front: Geoff Marks, Scott Macdonald, George Macgregor. Above: USA get their Walker Cup revenge at St Andrews in 1975. Back row (l to r) Gerry Koch, Jay Haas, Dr Edward Updegraff (capt), Bill Campbell, Dick Siderowf, George Burns, Curtis Strange, Craig Stadler. Front: John Grace, Jerry Pate, Marvin Giles. Right: Peter Thomson gets a little too close to the Swilcan Burn

Playing the course The Old Course, like the other three courses at St Andrews, is a public course, open to all. However, the tremendous demands made on the course have required some restrictions. The course is closed on Sundays. Members of the Royal and Ancient Golf Club have priority on the tee at specific times in August and September. From April to October, a ballot system is applied for starting times. And from time to time the Old Course may be entirely closed for a few weeks in the late winter or early spring.

Applications for reserved tee times should be made to the Secretary, Links Management Committee of St Andrews, Golf Place, St Andrews KY16 9JA, tel St Andrews (0334) 75757, not less than eight weeks in advance of the date of play. Reservations are not made for Saturdays and Thursday afternoons. Single players may not reserve a starting time or enter the ballot, although they may be allowed to play at the Starter's discretion. Fourball medal play is not permitted and applications for reserved times and entry to the ballot are accepted only on this understanding. There are no restrictions on ladies' play.

Adjoining courses These are the New, Jubilee, and Eden. All of them maintain to some degree the character of the Old – many people consider the New to be at least as difficult – and together they make a marvellous golfing complex.

New 6604 yards SSS 72   Eden 5971 yards SSS 69   Jubilee 6284 yards SSS 70

Recommended courses in the surrounding area There are many first-class courses in Fife; strongly recommended are Lundin Links, Ladybank, Elie and Crail. The Carnoustie and Gleneagles courses and Rosemount are also within reasonable reach of St Andrews.

Lundin GC, Golf Road, Lundin Links, Fife; tel Lundin Links (0333) 320202.
Ladybank GC, Annsmuir, Ladybank, Fife; tel Ladybank (0337) 30320.
Golf House Club, Elie, Fife; tel Elie (0333) 330327.
Crail Golfing Society, Balcomie Clubhouse, Crail, Fife; tel Crail (03335) 278.

Where to stay St Andrews and the surrounding area offers plenty of accommodation, and if possible visitors should spend at least one night in this splendid old university town.

Old Course Hotel, Old Station Road, St Andrews, Fife KY16 9SP; tel St Andrews (0334) 74371, telex 76280.
Rufflets Hotel, Strathkines Road, St Andrews, Fife; tel St Andrews (0334) 72594.
Scores Hotel, The Scores, St Andrews, Fife; tel St Andrews (0334) 72451.
Rusacks Marine Hotel, St Andrews, Fife; tel St Andrews (0334) 74321.

Simon Owen in trouble at the 17th in the final round of the 1978 Open. At the end he finished two strokes behind his playing partner and the eventual winner, Jack Nicklaus

St Andrews